MW00613974

THE SOUND
MIRROR

FLOOD EDITIONS
CHICAGO

THE SOUND MIRROR

ANDREW JORON

Copyright © 2008 by Andrew Joron All rights reserved Published by Flood
Editions www.floodeditions.com ISBN 978-0-9787467-8-0 Designed by
Quemadura Printed on acid-free, recycled paper in the United States of
America This book was made possible in part through a grant from the Illi-
nois Arts Council Many of these poems (or versions thereof) have appeared
previously in the following journals: English Language Notes, Fascicle, Green Inte-
ger Review, Hambone, Melancholia's Tremulous Dreadlocks, New American Writing, The
Modern Review, Practice: New Writing + Art, Skanky Possum, Talisman, Ur-Vox, and Volt.
Thanks to their editors. FIRST EDITION

HERE
EROS, A ROSE
AROSE, HER
 SOUND SO WOUND—

POUR RROSE, ENCORE ET TOUJOURS

THE SOUND MIRROR

THE MIRROR SOUND

Penned *A*
Cage confined
To page—

Lit, upon unlit lot, the
Letter
    O

—wrong sun, rung reason of

    One, that avatar of two. To
    One, who won't won't want—

    Here
O is I's

    avowal, a dead deed.
A gain to negate no gate.

So just my jest, my
Vote to *mon oeuvre*:

vroom over room & verity, the

Straight arriving
 late to
Strayed, a raid upon the rayed.

I AM THE DOOR

I, my
    being to begin, my die
To decide my deicide, am

Gone again to distance, & sand, & stand

    by fear
Entranced before the door.

Or do I travel as travail of a veil?

This science
Is that séance of the shore, the unsure.

All word-dawn
    is downward, so I raise
Reason to look to lack.

No & no, where the word runs red—

No (cure for suffering): no (furious core).

Because cause
    is curled
In a burning world—
    fact is also
    act, a faked effect.

Call of the best beast, as mind is moaned—

As one commands the other.

    The news comes wrapped
    already ripped.

    (The system of a mystery
Threw this through that.)

ASSUMPTION, THE

Climb, the
Premise, the—

What drama
    of the size of signs, of sighs
Seized at zero.

A dry soul is best
    because combustible—

But to stand
    beyond witness, burying the sun

    or else writing fire
    along a circumference of unclosing

—this is my faith & my reason.

I enter history
As a secret agent or stone effigy

dedicated to communism
but eaten away by music.

My chorus
    vacuum-crowded, I
    beg to begin—

    If now
    is a precipice, then
A human voice predates the universe.

Everything sends, never to receive
This message

Premonitory to a shriek—of
Shredded
    immensité the vocable, irrevocable
    Proof.

MATERIALISM

Failed fold
    makes the cut continuous—

Unclosed is
Unclothed
    in the drama that Thou art

    outward the word (outside

      —interstellar costume—

    the fits of a dress).
Unrepeating pattern

    where
X relaxes relation, where

X licks the elixir of
    night's rhyme with light.

Possessor, picture
Bare chamber—
 stain instead of identity—

 the plait of, the plaint of

 simple.

Thou thousand, imitation
Shadow.

AUTUMNAL SPRING

Written on a rotten
Leaf, word to ward *toward*:

the fallen are the
first to enter time.

Rived
The arrived, torn
The born.

Belated that
relation, floated upon flesh, as

Age to page: for the anatomy of reason
Is want.

(As the mire wants, taunts the mirror

or the scarf of the skin is
loosed in wind, in mind.)

—that we, that tree that travels

In unearthly season, bring breath to term—

To song, to sing "There is no
Belonging."

& "Belonging
Elongates to longing & the gates of song."

VOICE OF EYE

FOR GUSTAF SOBIN, A CONFESSION

(ON METHOD)

*A*ir is merest modulation to *err*

—to entertain the world, the
    ablest is A
Man of dark device.

His theater: shown blast, shone blind.

    To
    ward blackest vox, he

Springs; in
    what white
Bounds expresses X.

Driven as A
Man arrives riven

    as draft of that fabric, that breath.

    *

A thought is a bone known by its shadow.

*

Never as always to ask
Voice of eye, expecting

space to turn inside out—

as distance stares hard into the sun.

No number feeling

The heaven-fled, the
flayed inherent in flesh.

*

As pure strain, the straight line consoles him.

*

My page, my abject skin, music-scored
I scan.

If two facing mirrors = infinity
Then I
    have seen the back of your head, Beauty Hunter.

    Deleted here, O enciphers the rose.

    If reading = rewriting, then
    writing is not equal to itself.

For a circle collects only—but cannot find—its first & last.

    *

Antecedent
    to time: Now announces its
Ark unsealed.

You (all) dream headless, your (collective)
Body
    sounding like a drum.

    Saying you in first person. Repeating you.

A sea of heads surrounds the idol.

    *

His hollow hull, that
Body to be
    wrought & rotted in the same instant.

Unblinded, blue
    sun affixed to blinding heaven
Reverses the terms of exile.
    So convulse.

Sound against language, Jerusalem.

Empire, to rhyme with
Fire, carries sound to the point of resistance.
As Babylon
    sends sounds to sands.

After A
Man
    sound fades faster than light.

FIVE INQUIRIES BEYOND SEQUENCE

1

Minus one, my word

    charred marker, as darker is
My starker sun.

My steps to be stopped
Under ache of their echo—

    as accord is twinned, a
Cord is twined

In lines that liken winter to summer—

    & blank lines to black.

For writing (the non-

    locality of)

looks blind
to the reader.

& more: in reading, war
is worn around the eyes.

2

That moment, arrow's
     monument—or marrow's—

That telling tolling, *the*
Future is the time of time.

3

In reverse, in

Reverence, the limit of ascending
Harmony is dissonance—

My tide
Processional toward a lunar shell:
    apprehension of that term.

4

To cite:

    the knot of not
Configured by Gustaf Sobin

Fastening nothing, but Unfastening—

Making language
Tangent upon the void's ovoid

    interval, the very predicate of music.

5

The straight
Line that enters its own center
  is the Circle.

  O, such erased
  riches, &
Spooled loops—

  Les spasmes de l'oracle: structure.

HOME UNKNOWN STONE

Shh, shh, surest measure—
One minute too minute.

The blue animal lies bleeding
On a field of stars.

No, no word-order to end well

      meaning indwelling—

What effort, merely
    to sob out its
    winter-substance!

Tag from fragment: a certain light
Cannot be cited
    in the Book that wants invisibility.

That which needs nothing to exist
Fixes accident, each

    marriage of the genitive:

Prayer-preliminary to the symmetries in trees.

INSIDE A RUINED OBSERVATORY

stone is ascendant.

Here the eye
    was stopped inside a star, as the self
    inside a scar.

Only a red leaf remains
To disprove the telescope.

Under the dome, the mind still turns
    as melancholic as mechanical.

Above, a ceiling-walker
Has left
    just one footprint, by angelic logic.

Perhaps there is nothing to say—blues
    advance into invisibilities.

Perhaps
    a mirror is the right receiver
    for these words without reference—

    acausal, they are always to come
    apart, depart

    shadow-freighted, rolling
    like waves recessive from the shore.

    Oceanic
    curve, cursive, curse.

Cold enters everything—
That quiet disquiet
    that refuses quotation.

    Softly, as in an evening sunrise.

THE POVERTY OF FACT

One lizard is less than one word.
Whose tongue unscrolls to taste the dust?

The walls of the mind are painted
Hot pink, the color of electricity.

Either aether or ore, the barrens accumulate.
Forgive me, I have not eaten today.

I am a talking picture, nothing more
Than a tissue wedged between ages of silence.

Frame by frame, the bus window
Animates the still desert.

By the roadside, the skull of Taurus whitens
Beaconwise—

Correspondent to the unspilled sky.
His horns are garlanded with wandering planets.

This evening in the plaza
Heaven is the guitar that plays itself.

Old church, a rubble patch. Stop here to venerate
The bloody stumps of the black cactus.

Canyon I call for no answer.
To be accurate, a man goes back to his ghost.

As the militia guards the volcano, so
Is necessity measured, against the will.

[HECHO EN MÉXICO, MAYO 2002]

WHITE CROWS
(VASTATION)

1

Let visible speak, as the exponent of
   divisible.
Here, voice is a kind of eye, whose
Masking is asking all of all.

Ave of Wave—

That word that stops in substance, a hollow hand
Collecting fate.

Accursed, accused, accounted
Is not
One, is
   unwon, the in-
Verse of void.

   Being / is
Shivering shadow

—the clock of the living, the cloud of the dead.

2

White crows, abandoning the carcass, carry
Away the secret—

First thirst, then
Burst is announced by

the bloody blooms, the scored sky.

Blue wounds, blue winds—
A sun-cracked crust, the No of the known, the
noun of noon.

3

After time
This split, speech-lit terrain
    displayed
    splayed torture—
Only
    frozen form is free
    of content, balancing blindness, zero-
    believing.

Father, mother, noise knows no news—

Vortext
    of earth's
    stricken instrument, revoicing
    a depthlessness, a deafness to

    that blue that blew.

4

At center's *stop here*: the
     crimson hole, scene of the crime—
What stone was
     stabbed to stay the name?

No (as falsifier, as

     twist between time): where forgiving

     assent (to
     the stars, to the stairs

Of ascent)
Becomes the purpose of a bell.

To listen, the very likeness of lack in locus Dei—

As shall is shallow, *utter Shell*, who to whom

is inherent to breath
as the longest, ghost-dolorous
Vibration—

Speaking out / the perspective of fall.

5

Major the gist of minor motion—
        minor the logic of or, or
Aether

        —where, in mimicry of cry
The referent cannot be found.

        Red-ember'd this
        bruise
Remembered: *the lost*
        child, the chambered nautilus.

The silence the seed to be said: No

        louder than allowed—

Low bifurcated
    Law, the ritual of morning.

Wake to shake the air, activating echo

    & vastation.

THE KEENING OF MY KNIVES

Dear doctor:
the truth, to be stated, to stay alive, cannot
equal itself.

Let quiet be quoted
by moonlit buildings, gongs of the Negative.

Alien
Elegy, dissolve of sugar.
Avian
In its release from the hand, the frameless
instant, the stop.

Of air of air of air of air of error.

As of clouds
Eternally clearing, unwriting
the hand.

Given
that one undressed of his flesh

drowns in reflection—
The hand goes blind to belief.

An intent to wield *wailed* spilled *space*, therefore

the world will end today.
Here, I invent
a purpose for slow language

—perhaps vertical, or vortical—
Whose turbulence bleeds
Black—

Whose writing looks like unlike silences.

Dear doctor: my signature, many-chambered
vacancy, remains asylum.

RIFT HABITAT

Why I seem same seam:
    mothered more than once, I
    rail to rule the reel of real.

My sum, some-
    thing
    massed as
    my nothing most mist––

Plangent the plunge, full-throated
    through
My mind-roofed rift.

I invent my inventory in
    inverted time, tangent

    to the sureness of my shore, & its
    voracious shining.

Rending as rendering—

The line, the river
    that has no mouth.

That row that rose: run down, round Sun—

    Moon the fullness of
    rune, the form of
    ruin, renewing.

The starry stops, ends
In themselves—

Shape poured empty
    that requires choirs.

The low to console, the high
    to conceal. The call to cancel.

All is all exception—

DUST OF DUSK: THE ARABESQUES

1

Flickering licks at the lacks, then
At the locks.

Toward—what floored—

or what
adored, &
many-doored &
Windowed:

For force, a
Hollow, a
Halo, a
Hole.

Report
apart, so
clothes

The unbidden body, as
    dissonances
    disclose:

My flag is the

Utility of my rag, the

    shadow-totality of my flesh.

What age, what carnage
    recovers
    soil of soul, the
    nerve of never, wedged in white?

Not a note but imperative: utter silence.

Fault or
    falter, the bared device. Flat altar, ideal
Face
    before depth, so deaf the death

    laid upon the table of my double.

2

The lacks
    under the sun
Rise to looks:

Sun the sightless One, whose lit
Iterations

Speak of of & of

    expenditure & chill—

Lost at last

Knowing nothing other
    than shimmer as position.

With cause, my contingent visage
Wears its verb
    & judgment:

To unsex the fixed center—

That which lacks, then looks
    between my eyes: my

    twin identities, where
    woman is a man of woe.

KLANG-FIGUR

FOR RUSTY MORRISON

As, as "a
    dog is barking, a bog
    is darkening," is
Truth of God, truth of God

    is subtracted.

    I know not
To nominate night.

Time tells my duty

    to the dateless:
    a tearing & a tearing.

I decline the word ending, the cloudless eye:
    X aches for existence.

Still the conclusion, unstill the shore.

So loosed, last is the first

    made fiercest, there
    where the war of One is won.

Blest blast:

To break or to brake
    the breathtaking instant—

To find only in all
    the unfounded

& rife fire, the
    detail of eternal day as delay.

ATOMS HAVE
THEIR HIVE

God, it is to be
    supposed that *Man is in pain.*

Spilt into split, as sigh unto scythe—

Pain is a red scarf
Freed from my body
    & whirled away, a skirl on the wind.

As atoms have their hive
In *have*—
I halve my half forever.

    For: for the maker
    mirrored = marred.

Rhyming *ever over, over ever*

    —quill & quell—

What leaf-turned book, what
    landscape
Read red
    wall of sky, red wall of womb?

A man of sorrows knows no series, so
The sore rose cannot come to sere ease.

Gift of the impossible:
    total fragment that includes only what excludes itself.

    Thus, this
Whisper supports space, as a rumor

    or a room lost within its exact locality.

But a sob neither does nor does not resemble a bell

& wants night & light at once.

TWO ORPHIC
POEMS

NIGHTSUN, SIGN

Red, unread, as Eurydice's indices—

Why Orpheus? Why encipher fire?

Let the violin's violence tell the turn of the tune—

All's involuted volume, light as heavy as heaven.

A foot after a bent verse, averse, but for Before.

A mind met out of time, the shared shard.

Necessary errancy. Push of apparition, ash of pure relation—

The content not content to spare the spirit.

What? Whiter water, arriving raving?

Strike ~~instrument~~, the *the* is too definite, too deaf to infinity.

To send is to end.

AS ENDING, SEND

O tome, O tomb, I hum a hymn to home, to whom.

Cast to type, I ride to return to my native, candescent nothing.

As now, as never, ever arriving over variance—

Is & is as any nerve's revery.

A shaken occasion, only to mind the signed. All letters to tally—

The leaders of, the looters of, all toil & tarry.

A world, perhaps word, is tipped on its side, & pitted with days.

How now to lament a man's late mentality, his night-knotted mantle—

To say, unsay: *son, sin, sign, sun,* so soon unseen?

As failure of, as fuel of all relation: le *la,* the self-relation of nothing.

Fecund cave—

BREATH, BRING NOTHING TO TERM

Ring
Wrong instead of *song*—

Sense not sense, but fatal interference.
Arc of
    the maker, the marker

Born in reverse:
The borrower, the rower from the frozen zero.

So cotillions of ice shall
    clatter to
Unsure closure: rare air or error

    cool to all call, all clash of clouds.

Wanting
One without outside

    —while knowing the turn of torn, the
    deviance of all device.

So reckoning is this
Night-wreck of the Sun, perception pointing

To its stoppages:

    still object &
    agile shadow.

Fluent fall to flow to Flower
    &
Lightning-littered letter.

Imagine, engine
The state in flames

    & black
    thoughts
Of the character of a cataract, roaring
    to assemble the mind's semblance to nothing.

TO EACH CORRESPONDENT TO SPEECH

What weight do I await?

I am afraid that
Room is empty, apart from meaning.

Often a cat is trapped in
    all the intricacies of its senses.

—this Paradise
Is a desert
    populated by pillars
    half-human, half-mineral.

    Sun ever sum
Where a term is wanting

    to be called to co-
    ordinates

Horizontal to reason & vertical to vertigo.

I am the house that inhabits me.

As a man is
Unsigned, more than
Mantle
    of his mind, there is no master.
The wall, as will, stands still.

Salve me, solve me: my chorus to each
Correspondent to speech.

So no is yet
Yes
    & my revealing my reveiling—

NO TELLING

Of *white* the
Eternal
Wait, the weightless—

Of *black* the blank.

Rung long, wrong writing—

Tone-blown row that rose to rays
To raze all saying.

O, unbidden eye I bind Abandon by!

    —one to more
    always Married—

Nation, shadow, *duende*
    shall dwell under shell
& sell
    & end &

    (O, blow below
Intending)

Mind
Blind
    governance of the
In-given void.

Meaning that
From state to statement
    the referent is afraid:

So no, & no alone
Is polar to all pull.

    So there
I strike, nowhere, the name of

    my rose-prosaic, my

Prostrate man
& that thought
    that respires spires.

Thread through *throat*, through
Threat, through *throne*—

Here is my hero, & here
My tale
    of his jeweled, jailed
    integer.

CITATIONS
FROM SILENCE

1

Blue, I blow now into the long age of language. (Who goes not, as guest of his own identity, inside a ghost?) In theory, the Absolute is either a wheel or a well.

What will will touch teach? (Eros erases errancy in an unsung tongue.)

Unquelled under question, under shout—

I lie low within the waves, the aves, the naves of a dreamt cathedral, my talking taking the clarity of cloud.

Mocking making, all befalls the alphabet.

FIRST SILENCE

"Silence waits for an answer."

"Silence, endlessly divided, equals one."

"Silence always means more than it says."

"The universal silence is open-mouthed."

2

To strum these strings is to remedy the dying chord, to read red corridors of echoic code.

Sky-scattered & matter-mothered, I mince my meaning, a mere puppet upon the parapet. (The mouth, a moth, is painted.)

Entering the crimson scroll, I crawl into my scrawl, intending both to rob & rub out its substance. As weeping statue of the future past (where I wear a robe of stone), a posture is belated postulate, & beauty is unbidden body.

Never now, never here: here I revise my eyes to hear the concert of the concept.

To them the theme, to us the failed fold. (The known no, no later than the letter: another ruse of reason.)

SECOND SILENCE

"Silence is an attribute of something, not nothing."

"Silence is the presence of nothing within something."

"In the silence of solitude, release; in the silence of a multitude, confinement."

"The Moon reflects the silence of the Sun."

3

Forced is first. For the rest, the fired forest is fairest.

By that morning born of mourning, to return to the torn—

Where was I? Where will I be? What syllable is always said & unsaid, slower than silence?

By the known, bone-owned thought: tone knelling & annulling tone.

Revere these reversing rivers, emptying into their sources. Man to mean the imperfect tense of moan, or moon. A measure of calm: the infinitesimal circumference of a vanishing point.

One eon: dust shower, untreated voice-event, introduction to time.

THIRD SILENCE

"Noise is original: silence has no history."

"Silence cannot move or be moved."

"Silence can move only beyond space itself."

"Silence, like poetry, is neither true nor false."

4

Fact is fact! A forged object: the fears ensphering N. Father-faker the folk-roar.

Kissed, at dusk, the sun-sign, that metal, that mental disk.

To the narrows, avatars of narrative! Wild unto willed, I will rot as I am wrought.

My track to trick, unfit for fate, footless & left aloft—

As phased phrase, the speaking (of) a specter: my essay on (my unsaying of) the Demon of Noon. Sun, that spokeless wheel, frightens me; the color of space collapses under its weight.

FOURTH SILENCE

"Le silence éternel de ces espaces infinis m'effraie."

"Silence needs no translation; in this, it resembles a scream."

"We learn to speak before we learn to be silent."

"Writing is the silencing of speech."

5

For the forever-verb of Reverb, rain ruin.

A cycle, a sickle. (Eyes knit what is not: white night.)

So soon sight unnerves; & the observer serves the obverse.

FIFTH SILENCE

"Ceaselessness, like silence, is always suspended at the Last."

"Silence weighs more than stone."

"Zero is the mathematical egg of silence."

"The eye makes space; the ear makes time; the mind makes silence."

6

I tries trace (the right root), if & only if self falsifies (kite caught in the trees). He who looked to locked room. Trace to entrance.

I's blindness bleeds to bells. To *here*, the banishment of sound. (To *round*, the bound of *ruined*.) Or mirror or mire, fire before ash.

All meaning about meaning (accepted but excepted X) cancels to reconcile.

End by and & end—

By words (the birds of startlement), by *salivating stars* (salvational), the very nations end, the destinations send themselves.

SIXTH SILENCE

"The Absolute Book will be composed of citations from silence."

"Silence is at once immediate and remote. Its middle is missing."

"Noise is not the antithesis of silence, but merely its most minor modification."

"Silence is interior to itself."

7

The sun, as sum, is less than one. Verse versus its wave-octave: *wrath, writhe, wreathe, wraith,* all cool to the call, the locality of a collective voice.

A prose to bare the skin of the mind, kind beyond kind: promiscuous scar, the promise of the rose. Rhyme to take to ache, the icon of time.

SEVENTH SILENCE

"Silence is the dwelling-place of speech, but speech is not the dwelling-place of silence."

"Silence opposes nothing, yet overcomes everything."

"There is only one silence."

"Silence is a thought rather than a thing."

8

The veil of vision, the curtain of condition. Invent, to lie over lie, a voice as vast & as vacant as silence.

One unwon. A bell or a ball turned inside out is a bowl; so the Whole is held, beggar-wise, no bigger than—

State & statement, star & startlement.

A dust to be steadied, as the *time of time* is studied. A fate fitted to the line's angelic angle, if then subjected to mood & tangle. The sentence is death, bare bones without weather.

Out of doubt, the way away, a window free from frame.

LAST SILENCE

"Neither distance nor time can attenuate the broadcast of silence."

"The form of silence is also the content of silence."

"Silence keeps its secret."

"Blast silence!"

ANDREW JORON

was born in San Antonio, Texas, in 1955 and grew up in Stuttgart, Germany; Lowell, Massachusetts; and Missoula, Montana. He attended the University of California at Berkeley, where he majored in history and philosophy of science. After a decade and a half spent writing science-fiction poetry, culminating in his volume *Science Fiction* (Pantograph Press, 1992), he began to elaborate other forms of lyric speculation. This work has been collected in *The Removes* (Hard Press, 1999) and in *Fathom* (Black Square Editions, 2003). *The Cry at Zero*, a selection of his prose poems and critical essays, was published by Counterpath Press in 2007. Joron is also the translator, from the German, of the Marxist-Utopian philosopher Ernst Bloch's *Literary Essays* (Stanford University Press, 1998). He lives in Berkeley, where he works as a part-time proofreader and indexer.